THIS BOOK BELONGS TO

Alison Peabhleen
Sovalku...

Published by BBC Books,
an imprint of BBC Worldwide Publishing.
BBC Worldwide Ltd., Woodlands, 80 Wood Lane, London W12 0TT

First published 1958 by Sampson Lowe

This edition 1992
Reprinted 1994, 1995
© Darrell Waters Limited 1958 as to all text and illustrations

Enid Blyton's signature mark and the word 'NODDY'
are Registered Trade Marks of Darrell Waters Limited

ISBN 0 563 36831 4

Printed in Great Britain by BPC Paulton Books Limited.

YOU'RE A GOOD FRIEND NODDY!

BY *Enid Blyton*

CONTENTS

1. A Letter for Noddy
2. The Day of the Party
3. What Happened at the Party
4. Where is Big-Ears?
5. Looking for Whiskers
6. The Wily Wizard
7. Big-Ears Finds Whiskers
8. Everything's Right Again!

BBC BOOKS

THE POSTMAN WALKED GLOOMILY DOWN THE FRONT PATH
THINKING OF ALL THE PARTIES HE WAS NEVER ASKED TO

1. A LETTER FOR NODDY

RAT-A-TAT-TAT!
"Why, that must be the postman!" said Noddy, in surprise. He was just getting up, so he wrapped a big towel round himself and ran to the door, his hair untidy and his feet bare.

"Letter for you, Noddy," said the postman. "I think it's from Big-Ears."

"Oh yes—it's his writing, isn't it?" said Noddy, looking at the envelope with big writing on it. "What do you suppose he says, Postman?"

"Look and see," said the postman, who was always interested in everybody's letters. So Noddy tore open the big envelope and found a large white card inside.

"Oooh, look, Postman!" he said. "Big-Ears is giving a party—and he's asked me to come. It's tomorrow! A party! Are *you* going, Postman?"

"No," said the postman, looking gloomy. "It's very sad, you know—I take invitations to parties almost every day—but nobody ever asks *me*."

"I'll ask you to my very next one," said Noddy, nodding his head fast. "I won't forget. Postman, did you take a letter to Tessie Bear as well?"

"Oh yes—and to the Tubby Bears next door, and to Miss Fluffy Cat, and the Wobbly Man," said the postman. "That's all. I don't really think Big-Ears could get any more into his house. And he's ordered a big cake. I know that because I took the postcard about it to the baker's yesterday."

"It must be nice to be a postman," said Noddy, "and know simply everything."

A LETTER FOR NODDY

"And it must be nice to be a taxi-man like you, and go everywhere," said the postman. "And on wheels too. I go on my feet, and it's a wonder they're not worn out."

"Well—I'm getting rather cold with only a towel on," said Noddy, suddenly feeling that the postman might go on talking all morning. "Good-bye." He went indoors, and the postman walked gloomily down the front path, thinking of

all the parties he was never asked to. Noddy saw him out of his window and felt sorry again. "I *really* will ask him to my next party!" he thought.

He put Big-Ears' card on his chimney-piece, where it looked rather grand. Noddy read it out loud.

YOU'RE A GOOD FRIEND NODDY!

"Please come to a little party at Toadstool House on Tuesday afternoon at four o'clock. Love from Big-Ears."

"I wonder why Big-Ears didn't tell me about it when I saw him last week," thought Noddy, as he dressed himself. "I suppose he thought of it very suddenly. I'm glad Tessie Bear and the Tubby Bears are going."

Mrs Tubby Bear called over the fence to Noddy when she saw him getting out his car.

"Noddy! Are you going to Big-Ears' party?"

"Oh *yes!* I had a card this morning," said Noddy, "and the postman said you had one too. Why is Big-Ears having a party all of a sudden, Mrs Tubby Bear?"

"I really don't know," she said. "But listen, Noddy, you can't go in that dirty shirt—you've spilt cocoa all down it!"

A LETTER FOR NODDY

"Dear me, so I have," said Noddy, looking down at his little red shirt.

"Well, you pass me all your clothes over the fence this evening," said Mrs Tubby Bear, "and I'll wash and iron them for you. And don't forget to brush your red shoes!"

"Oh, you *are* kind," said Noddy. "I'll take you up to Big-Ears' house in my car tomorrow, Mrs Tubby Bear, and then I'll go back and fetch Tessie Bear. I won't take the Wobbly Man because he can never sit down."

Noddy went off happily in his car. How nice it was to have a party to think about. "I hope there'll be balloons," he thought. "And a cake with candles on. Oh no—it won't be a birthday party, of course, because Big-Ears had his birthday a little while ago. Oh, I *do* love a party!"

And Noddy sang a party song as he drove

YOU'RE A GOOD FRIEND NODDY!

along, much to the surprise of Sally Skittle, Mr Plod and Miss Fluffy Cat, who were all walking down the road.

"Oh what shall I eat at the party?
Oh WHAT shall I eat at the party?
I think I will start
With a little jam tart,
And then I will take
A big slice of cake,
And a chocolate bun
(But only just one),
And a jelly that shakes
And quivers and quakes,
And some lemonade too,
And a biscuit or two,
And . . . well, I am sure
I can't eat any more!
That's what I'll eat at the party,
Yes, that's what I'll eat at the party!"

2. THE DAY OF THE PARTY

MRS TUBBY BEAR looked over the fence that night. "Bring me your dirty clothes!" she called to Noddy.

"Coming!" said Noddy, and came out of his door with a pile of clothes over his arm. He was wearing his dressing-gown, and Mrs Tubby Bear thought he looked a dear little fellow.

"I'll wash them tonight, and hang them on the line to dry, and iron them first thing in the morning," she said. "And you'll have to be VERY careful not to get them dirty tomorrow, Noddy."

"Oh, I will," said Noddy, nodding his head. "You *are* kind, dear Mrs Tubby."

YOU'RE A GOOD FRIEND NODDY!

Next morning Noddy put on his dressing-gown again and went to fetch his clothes. Mrs Tubby Bear handed them to him, all beautifully clean and smelling of her nice soap. He gave her a hug.

"I'll call for you just before four o'clock," he said, "and take you and Mr Tubby up to Big-Ears' house." And away he went to get dressed.

He was very careful not to get dirty that day. He nearly forgot once when a funny noise came from underneath his car, and he got out to see to it. He was just about to crawl under the car when he remembered his nice clean clothes.

"I'm afraid I can't see to you today, little car," he said, getting back into his seat. "So if you've got something wrong, you'll just have to put up with it."

"Parp-parp," said the car, softly, and didn't make any more noises. Noddy soon picked up a passenger who wanted to go to the market to do his shopping. It was one of the wooden soldiers from the fort, holding a gun over his shoulder.

"Your gun is sticking into my hat," said Noddy. So the soldier put it down by his foot. "Now it's sticking

"YOUR GUN'S STICKING INTO MY HAT," SAID NODDY TO THE WOODEN SOLDIER

YOU'RE A GOOD FRIEND NODDY!

into my shoe," said Noddy, and he pushed the gun away. BANG! It went off, and the car gave such a jump that Noddy and the soldier almost fell out. Noddy's hat flew off into the mud, and he was very cross.

"What made you let off your gun?" he said. "Look at my hat, it's all muddy—and I'm going to a party today!"

"Well, *you* let it off," said the soldier. "You hit the trigger when you pushed it away. Quick—don't let's quarrel about it. Here comes Mr Plod to see what the shooting is about!"

THE DAY OF THE PARTY

Sure enough, Mr Plod was hurrying towards them, wondering what little Noddy was up to *now*. Letting off guns in the street—really, whatever next!

Noddy shot off at top speed, and the soldier's hat blew off. "Hey, stop—*my* hat's gone now," he cried.

"Well—Mr Plod will pick it up and keep it for you," said Noddy, with a giggle. "You can go and collect it on the way back."

The soldier didn't like the idea of that at all. "I shan't pay you for this ride!" he said, fiercely. "First you set off my gun, then I lose my hat."

"All right. You needn't pay me," said Noddy. "You do look funny without your hat! Look, here is the market. Hurry up and get out, because I can see someone else wanting me."

YOU'RE A GOOD FRIEND NODDY!

It was a clockwork clown. He got into the car and Noddy drove him to the station.

"Could you wind me up please, Noddy," he said. "I think my clockwork is running down, and I don't want to miss my train."

So Noddy wound him up—clickity-clickity-click. "There you are," said Noddy. "Hurry up now—here comes that train!"

The clown paid Noddy sixpence for the ride, and a penny for winding him up. Noddy drove away

to look for more passengers. It was a busy day and plenty of people wanted to hire his little red-and-yellow car.

Noddy kept thinking of Big-Ears' party. "I wish he'd asked me three or four days ago," thought

THE DAY OF THE PARTY

Noddy. "It's so nice to have something to look forward to for *days*. I've only had yesterday and today to think about it. Oh, what shall I eat at the party? I think I will start with a little jam tart, and then . . ."

"Hey, clockwork mouse," he shouted. "Take your tail out of the road. Do you want it run over?"

The clockwork mouse was standing on the edge of the pavement talking to Sally Skittle. He had forgotten all about his long tail. He swished it quickly off the road, and Noddy drove on, thinking that clockwork mice were really rather stupid, *always* forgetting about their tails!

At three o'clock Noddy went back to his little house to wash and tidy himself for the party.

YOU'RE A GOOD FRIEND NODDY!

He did look nice and clean and tidy when he went to call for Mr and Mrs Tubby Bear. They were waiting for him. Little Tubby Bear was crying.

"I want to come too! Noddy's going. Why can't I come?"

"Well, last time you went to tea with Big-Ears you pulled his cat's tail," said Mrs Tubby. "And it rushed out and didn't come back that night. I'm not surprised you haven't been asked if that is the way you behave."

They left Tubby behind, a sad, fat little bear, with tears pouring down his furry nose and dripping round his feet. Noddy felt quite sorry for him.

He drove Mr and Mrs Tubby up to Big-Ears' Toadstool House and then went to fetch Tessie Bear. She was ready too, standing outside the front gate. From inside the house came the sound of angry barking.

"That's the Bumpy-Dog," said Tessie, as they drove off. "He hasn't been asked to the party, of course, because of Big-Ears' cat, and he's very

TUBBY WAS LEFT BEHIND WITH TEARS POURING DOWN HIS FURRY NOSE

YOU'RE A GOOD FRIEND NODDY!

annoyed. He hasn't licked me once today, he's so upset."

"Well, that's a good thing anyway," said Noddy, who thought Bumpy was the lickiest dog he had ever known. "Here we are, Tessie. Now for a wonderful party. I DO wonder why Big-Ears is giving it, don't you?"

3. WHAT HAPPENED AT THE PARTY

BIG-EARS came to welcome them at the door. "You're the last!" he said. "Tessie, you do look nice in your party frock! Come along in!"

Noddy and Tessie went into the Toadstool House and it seemed quite crowded, because there were already four people there—the Tubby Bears, Miss Fluffy Cat, and the Wobbly Man. Sitting on a velvet cushion on a little table all to itself was Big-Ears' big black cat. It purred very loudly indeed.

"Ooooh—doesn't Whiskers look grand today, Big-Ears!" said Noddy, in surprise. "Look at the lovely red ribbon round his neck—he's a very *purry* cat this afternoon, isn't he?"

"Well, it's his birthday, so he ought to feel purry!" said Big-Ears. "He's such a nice cat that I thought I'd give a party for him. That's why I asked you all to come today."

"Oh! Many happy returns of the day, Whiskers!" cried everyone, and Tessie stroked him till he purred like a bubbling kettle. Noddy thought of a birthday song at once. He sang it to the cat, who was very, very pleased.

"Oh, Birthday Cat,
I'll sing you a song,
Your eyes are green, and your tail is long.
You have a coat
All soft and furry,
And a voice that's nice and purry.
Your whiskers too
Are very fine,
I sometimes wish that they were mine!
Oh, Birthday Cat,
This song's for you,
So PLEASE be happy all day through!"

"That's a nice song," said Big-Ears. "I wish I could sing songs like you, Noddy. Well, what about sitting down and having our tea? I'm afraid *you'll* have to stand, Mr Wobbly Man, but you won't mind that, will you?"

WHAT HAPPENED AT THE PARTY

"Not a bit—I can easily wobble round the table and help myself," said the Wobbly Man, and he reached out to take a large piece of cake.

"He wobbles and gobbles,
He sways to and fro,"
began Noddy, but Big-Ears frowned at him. "No, Noddy. That song sounds a bit rude," he said. "Mrs Tubby Bear, do have a piece of this jam sponge. I made it myself, and my cat stirred the mixture for me."

"Meow," said the cat, proudly.

YOU'RE A GOOD FRIEND NODDY!

"Isn't Whiskers going to have any tea?" asked Tessie Bear.

"Well, he's having a tin of sardines with cream poured over them after we've finished," said Big-Ears. "I didn't think you'd like the look of it while you were  having *your* tea. Anyway, he likes to sit there and blink at us. He's a wonderful cat. I'm so very fond of him. I don't know what I should do without him."

"I know. I feel rather like that about the Bumpy-Dog now," said Tessie, taking a chocolate bun. "I know he's bumpy and jumpy and licky and barky, but he is *so* loving, and he would do anything in the world for me. I shut him up before I came here, of course, and I know he will be as good as gold and stay there quietly till I . . ."

She stopped suddenly. Everyone lifted their

WHAT HAPPENED AT THE PARTY

heads and listened. Surely—surely that wasn't a bark in the distance? The cat stood up at once, all its fur rising up in anger.

The barking came nearer. And then, good gracious me, someone flung himself against the door. It flew open—and in gambolled the Bumpy-Dog, smiling all over his face! He had come to the party too! Whiskers gave a flying

leap and disappeared out of the window in a flash. Bumpy leapt after him—and landed in the middle of the tea-table. Oh dear, oh dear, oh dear!

Splashes of lemonade! Bits of cake all over the place! Biscuits flying through the air! A jam tart landing on the Wobbly Man's head! What a to-do there was!

Big-Ears was very, very angry. He stormed at the Bumpy-Dog, shouting in such a loud voice that little Tessie Bear was frightened.

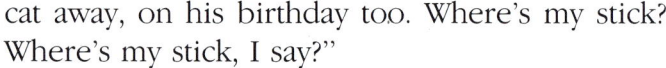

"You weren't asked to the party! You've frightened my cat away, on his birthday too. Where's my stick? Where's my stick, I say?"

The Bumpy-Dog didn't understand that he had spoilt the party. He was sure everyone would be just as pleased to see him as he was to see them. He went round jumping up and licking everyone lovingly.

He was most surprised to see how the Wobbly Man wobbled about when he leapt at him. He thought this was great fun, and kept jumping at the Wobbly Man to make him wobble to and fro. Then Big-Ears found his stick.

WHAT HAPPENED AT THE PARTY

Whack! What a dreadful shock for the Bumpy-Dog! He yelped and ran straight out of the house. Then he came back and looked mournfully through the window. Tessie began to cry.

But Big-Ears was cross with Tessie, too! "You couldn't have shut that dog up properly!" he said, angrily. "It was very careless of you!"

"Don't you talk to Tessie like that, Big-Ears," said, Noddy, fiercely. "I'm ashamed of you. Come along, Tessie, I'll take you home!"

And Noddy hurried little Tessie Bear to his car and drove her quickly home. He gave her a hug and she cheered up.

"I'm going back to Big-Ears' house to fetch the Tubby Bears," he said. "Don't cry any more. It wasn't your fault, Tessie. Oh dear—what a horrid end to a lovely party!"

4. WHERE IS BIG-EARS?

ALL the other guests had begun walking home, except the Wobbly Man who wobbled, of course. Noddy met them in his car.

"I shall never, NEVER go to see Big-Ears again," he said, and he really meant it. He was cross all that evening, and all the next day and the next.

And then he began to wonder if Big-Ears' cat had come back. Whiskers really was a very nice cat, and Big-Ears was so fond of him. He said Whiskers stopped him from feeling lonely at night.

WHERE IS BIG-EARS?

So on the third day after the party Noddy drove his car up to the Toadstool House. It was shut, and there was a notice on the door. "GONE AWAY TO LOOK FOR MY POOR OLD CAT."

Oh dear! So the cat *hadn't* come back. Noddy saw a small rabbit peeping round a tree. "Hey, Bunny! Which way did Big-Ears go? Do you know?"

"That way, early this morning," said the rabbit, pointing. "He was crying, Noddy. He was crying so hard that he couldn't see his way very well, and he rode his bicycle straight into a tree and bumped his head."

"Oh *dear!*" said Noddy. "Fancy Big-Ears crying! I can't believe it. I feel rather like crying myself now. Well— I'm going after Big-

Ears. If he's unhappy he needs a friend, and I'm his friend and he's mine."

So off he went down the woodland path that the rabbit had showed him. "Parp-parp!" Even Noddy's car sounded down in the dumps. "Over the

YOU'RE A GOOD FRIEND NODDY!

bumps, down in the dumps, over the bumps, down in the dumps," rattled the wheels. Noddy drove on and on and on.

"I ought to catch up with Big-Ears soon," he thought. "A bicycle doesn't go nearly as fast as a car. Ah—here's someone to ask about him. Hey, little doll!"

A little golden-haired doll looked round. "Have you seen an old, old brownie in a red hat?" asked Noddy. She smiled and pointed down a little lane.

"Yes. He went down there, look. He asked me the way to Toy-Cat Town."

"Good gracious!" said Noddy, driving off. "I suppose he's heard that his cat has gone to live there. Well, I'll soon catch him up."

WHERE IS BIG-EARS?

He caught up with Big-Ears round the very next corner! He saw someone sitting by the side of the road. His bicycle was lying on its side, all twisted.

Noddy drove up and jumped out of his car in fright. "Big-Ears! Are you hurt? Big-Ears, what's happened?"

Big-Ears looked up and was most astonished to see Noddy.

"Hallo!" he said. "No, I'm not hurt. I fell off my bicycle when it went over a big stone. I'm afraid it's a bit damaged. I'm looking for my poor old cat."

"I've come to help you," said Noddy. "I'll

YOU'RE A GOOD FRIEND NODDY!

take you to Toy-Cat Town. Let's put your bicycle on the back of the car, and we'll drive off together."

"Noddy, you are very, very kind," said Big-Ears, and he smiled for the first time. Noddy couldn't help hugging him.

"Now you get in," he said. "We'll soon find dear old Whiskers. I'm very sorry he had such a fright, Big-Ears."

"Yes. So am I," said Big-Ears. "And I'm sorry I was cross with dear little Tessie Bear. I keep on thinking about how I made her cry, and I feel so unhappy about it."

"Well—you can give her a hug and a kiss when you see her next," said Noddy. "Then everything will be all right. Come along—off to Toy-Cat Town we go!"

And away they went at top speed, with Big-Ears' bicycle jiggling away at the back.

5. LOOKING FOR WHISKERS

IT wasn't very far to Toy-Cat Town. Noddy drove into it very slowly, on the look-out for Big-Ears' old cat.

"It should be easy to find Whiskers," said Noddy, "because all he wears is a big red bow round his neck. He isn't dressed up as these toy cats are."

He stopped beside a very grand cat, dressed in check trousers, a green coat, and a top hat.

"Could you tell me if you have seen a quite *ordinary* cat here?" asked Noddy. "A cat that only says 'meow' or 'purr-purr' or 'hiss-hiss'."

YOU'RE A GOOD FRIEND NODDY!

"I don't know any ordinary cats," said the toy cat scornfully. "Certainly none that say 'hiss-hiss'. But I did see a common-looking black cat running through here on four paws yesterday—*on four paws!* Fancy that! He didn't even know how to walk properly! I can tell you, he wouldn't be allowed to stay *here* long!"

Big-Ears went red in the face, and looked angry. "Let me tell you this, you silly high-and-mighty cat..." he began. But Noddy wouldn't let him quarrel with a toy cat.

He drove on at once, with Big-Ears grumbling away into his whiskers.

He stopped beside a dear little kitten-cat in a bonnet and spotty dress.

"Hallo, Kitten-Cat!" said Noddy, his head

LOOKING FOR WHISKERS

nodding hard. "Have you seen a large black cat running along on four paws?"

"Oh yes!" said the kitten-cat, looking at Noddy with big, wide eyes. "He was on the way to Wizard Town. I expect he wanted to go and live with a wizard and help him with his magic spells. Black cats are good at that, you know."

Big-Ears groaned. "Wizard Town! We'll never find him there. Oh my poor old cat! I do hope he's *still* a cat and not turned into a black beetle or anything."

Noddy looked alarmed. "Oh, surely that couldn't happen!" he said. "Thank you, Kitten-Cat, you've helped us."

The toy kitten waved to them and went on her

way. Noddy drove on, and soon came to a signpost. One arm said: "OVER THERE". Another one said: "NOT FAR OFF". The third one said: "WIZARD TOWN".

"Well, that's the way to go," said Noddy, and swung his car to the left. Off they went again. It was quite a long way to Wizard Town.

"That must be it," said Noddy at last, pointing to some high towers that seemed to rise up to the clouds. "I don't like wizards much, Big-Ears. Do you?"

"I don't mind them at all," said Big-Ears. "I can always get the better of any wizard—so you needn't worry, Noddy. Hurry up now—I do so want to find my dear old cat."

They came into Wizard Town, and Noddy drove carefully through the long, curving street. Goodness, what a lot of towers there were! Their square or pointed tops rose right to the clouds.

"I say—look at that shop!" said Noddy, stopping so suddenly that Big-Ears' hat slid down on his nose. "It's full of black cats."

So it was! Behind the window

NODDY STOPPED SO SUDDENLY THAT BIG-EARS' HAT
SLID DOWN ON HIS NOSE

were a great many fine black cats, all with the greenest of green eyes. A card in the window said: "BLACK CATS FOR SALE. GOOD FOR HELP IN MAKING SPELLS. NEEDED BY EVERY WIZARD. ENQUIRE INSIDE."

"Come along quickly. We'll see if my dear old

Whiskers is there!" said Big-Ears, and he jumped out of the car so suddenly that he nearly knocked over a wizard in a long flyaway cloak, sprinkled with stars. The wizard cried out angrily and raised his long wand as if he were going to make a spell over Big-Ears. But Big-Ears reached up, took his wand and broke it in half!

"Don't you try any tricks on *me*," he said.

LOOKING FOR WHISKERS

"I'm Big-Ears the brownie from Toadstool Wood, and I can teach you more spells than you've ever dreamed of!"

Whooooosh! The wizard disappeared at once in a puff of smoke! He was afraid of Big-Ears. Noddy stared in surprise and alarm. "I don't think I like this kind of thing," he said to Big-Ears.

Big-Ears took no notice. He looked very determined indeed. He walked into the cat shop and rapped on the counter. A small goblin came running in, bowing.

"I've come about a cat," said Big-Ears. "Show me all you have!"

6. THE WILY WIZARD

WELL, what a collection of cats there was in that shop! Big and small, fat and thin, long-tailed and short-tailed. Every one of them had bright green, gleaming eyes. One put out a quick paw and scratched Noddy.

"Don't," said Noddy, crossly. "If I were a wizard I'd never choose *you!*"

"The cat I'm looking for isn't here," said Big-Ears, sadly. "Did you have a new one in yesterday or the day before?"

"We had one yesterday," said the goblin, shooing the cats back into the window. "He was big and fat, with a smart red bow, and . . ."

"That's the one! That's my cat!" cried Big-Ears in delight. "Where is he now?"

"Let me see," said the goblin, opening a

THE WILY WIZARD

big, shining book, and running his finger down a column marked CATS. "Ah yes—the Wily Wizard bought him—for sixpence."

"*Sixpence!* But he is worth a fortune!" cried Big-Ears, angrily. "Sixpence! I never heard of such a thing."

"Well, the cat didn't seem to mind," said the goblin, grinning. "He went off with old Wily, purring like anything. That's the nineteenth cat the Wily Wizard has had."

"What happened to the other cats?" said Big-Ears, astonished.

"Oh, various things," said the goblin. "When spells go wrong, you know, anything may happen to the cat. One turned into a mouse and ran down a mouse-hole. But it still kept its mew, so no other mouse would be friends with it. And another time a cat made a mistake in a spell and shot off to the moon. I saw it go by in the air—whizzz!"

"I don't like this at all," said Big-Ears, very worried. "Noddy, we'll have to find Whiskers at once. Where does the Wily Wizard live, goblin?"

YOU'RE A GOOD FRIEND NODDY!

"See that hill?" said the goblin, pointing. "Well, there's a house there with a tower—you can see it shining from here. That's where old Wily lives. But be careful of him. He's a tricky one, as wily as his name."

"I'm a match for any wizard," said Big-Ears and tramped out of the shop looking worried again.

"Drive to the Wily Wizard's, Noddy," he said. "And be quick. I don't want to see my old cat whizzing off to the moon at any minute. Oh dear—WHY did that Bumpy-Dog have to frighten him away like that? What a dog!"

They drove to the Wily Wizard's house and stopped outside. Big-Ears hooted loudly, "Parp-parp-PARP!"

Someone looked out of the window. It was the Wily Wizard, rather small and bent, with very sharp eyes indeed. He came running out.

"Who are you? Is this your car? I've always wanted a car like this," he said. "Let me have a ride. Let me drive it myself. Ooooh, is this the horn?" Parp-parp. "What a wonderful car. Do let me drive. I can . . ."

"Wait a minute, *wait* a minute," said Big-Ears,

44

"WHO ARE YOU? IS THIS YOUR CAR? I'VE ALWAYS WANTED A CAR LIKE THIS," EXCLAIMED THE WILY WIZARD

YOU'RE A GOOD FRIEND NODDY!

pushing the wizard away from the car. "I've come to . . ."

"Oh, I *hope* you've come to sell me the car," said the wizard. "I hope you have. Just what I want. Oh what a beauty, and just listen to the horn too!" Parp-parp-parp.

"Don't keep tooting the horn!" said Big-Ears crossly. "AND STOP TALKING. *I* want to talk to you, I . . ."

"Well, talk away, my good fellow, talk away,' said the wizard, tooting the horn again. He pushed Noddy out and sat in the driving seat. "Just the right size for me. I never saw such a fine little car. It's wonderful, wonderful. I

THE WILY WIZARD

tell you, brownie, it's just what I've been looking for, and I'll . . ."

"If you don't stop talking and listen to me I'll put a spell on you and turn you into a record-player," shouted Big-Ears. "I WANT TO KNOW WHERE MY CAT IS!"

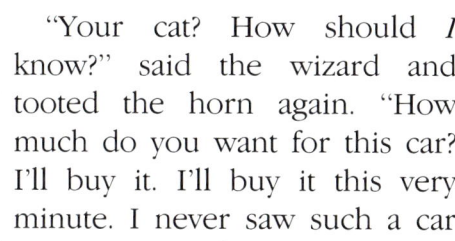

"Your cat? How should *I* know?" said the wizard and tooted the horn again. "How much do you want for this car? I'll buy it. I'll buy it this very minute. I never saw such a car in my life, it's the very . . ."

"Noddy, stay here and see that he doesn't try to drive the car away," said Big-Ears, in despair. "I'm going into the house to look for my cat."

YOU'RE A GOOD FRIEND NODDY!

He left the wizard talking non-stop to Noddy, and ran into the house. There was one enormous room inside, with a blue-flamed fire burning in the middle. Round it sat five cats, watching the flames. But not one of them was Big-Ears' cat.

"What spell is this?" asked

Big-Ears, astonished, as the flames changed to green. Little silver balls began to rise in the air and then fell back into the flames with the sound of tiny bells.

The cats stared at him and didn't answer. Their green eyes shone like small lamps. Then, as he

THE WILY WIZARD

watched, they all stood up, arched their backs, and marched solemnly round the strange fire. Then they sat down again.

"Well, I hope my cat has something better to do than march round a silly green fire," said Big-Ears, and went to a steep, curving flight of stairs that led up into the tall pointed tower.

"Sssss-sssss-sssss!" hissed all the cats, looking at Big-Ears as if to warn him.

"Oh—so you don't want me to go up the stairs?" said Big-Ears. "Why not? Well, I'm going!" And up the stone stairway he went, two steps at a time!

7. BIG-EARS FINDS WHISKERS

"WHISKERS! Puss, puss! Where's my old cat?" called Big-Ears, as he tore up the stairs. And almost at once he heard an answer!

"MEE-OW! MEE-OW-EE-OW!" Big-Ears opened a door, and there, sitting beside another fire, this time one with purple flames, was dear old Whiskers, all alone. He sprang up on Big-Ears' shoulder, and purred, and rubbed his head against his face.

"Oh, my dear old Whiskers! Oh, my fat, furry old friend!" said Big-Ears, two big tears running down his cheeks. The cat licked them away with a small, pink tongue. He purred again and rubbed his head lovingly against Big-Ears.

BIG-EARS FINDS WHISKERS

"You'll come home with me, won't you, Whiskers?" said Big-Ears. "Come along then. We'll go back and give *another* party—and if Bumpy-Dog ever dares frighten you again I'll turn myself into an *enormous* dog and chase him! Come along—Noddy's waiting outside."

So down they went, the cat in Big-Ears' arms, still purring loudly. All the cats round the fire

looked up in surprise. One began to say "ME-OW-EE-OW" very loudly, but just then the time came for them all to march solemnly round the fire again. It had little stars jumping out of it now, and one cat was catching them in a box.

YOU'RE A GOOD FRIEND NODDY!

"Very clever," said Big-Ears. "But my cat's not going to learn tricks like that. He's clever at catching mice—and that's all *I* care about!"

He walked out to the car and Noddy gave a squeal of delight when he saw the big cat in Big-Ears' arms.

"You've found him! Oh, good, Big-Ears! I'm so glad. Can you get the wizard out of my car? I can't get a word in—he's been talking all the time you've been gone. Just listen to him."

"And I suppose it doesn't use much petrol," the wizard was saying, "and doesn't need much cleaning. Yes, and I can easily make a garage for it to sleep in, I know a spell for that."

"Get out, please, and let me get in," said Big-Ears. "I want to take my cat home."

BIG-EARS FINDS WHISKERS

"*Your* cat! What nonsense!" cried the wizard, suddenly seeing the cat. "He's mine. I bought him for sixpence—and he wasn't worth it, either. He doesn't even know how to watch a spell! I'm in the middle of training him. You put that cat down, or I'll turn him into an elephant.

Then you'd find it difficult to carry him home. Ha ha!"

"You will not do anything of the sort," said Big-Ears, fiercely.

"Oh, I will, I will!" said the wizard, and to Noddy's dismay he chanted a few curious words—and goodness gracious, a little elephant's trunk began to grow out of the cat's nose!

YOU'RE A GOOD FRIEND NODDY!

"No, no!" cried Big-Ears. "Stop! I won't have my cat turned into an elephant, or anything else either. Here's sixpence. That's what you paid for him!"

"No. I'm not selling him," said the wizard. "But I'll *exchange* him for something else I want."

"What is it you want? I'll give you *anything*—even my Toadstool House—or my bicycle," said Big-Ears.

"Pooh! I don't want those!" said the wizard. "No. Give me this little *car*, and you can have your cat."

"NO. CERTAINLY NOT!" shouted Noddy, and he pushed the wizard right out of the car—bump! Wily jumped up, grabbed the cat from Big-Ears and ran indoors.

Big-Ears looked so shocked and upset that Noddy couldn't bear it. He rushed after the wizard.

BIG-EARS FINDS WHISKERS

"You can have my car. You can have it. Let Big-Ears have his cat!"

Well! What do you think of *that?* Big-Ears could hardly believe it. Generous little Noddy! Kind, unselfish Noddy! Big-Ears couldn't think of enough nice things to say about him!

The Wily Wizard came back, smiling all over his face. He handed the cat to Big-Ears. Big-Ears solemnly gave the wizard sixpence, much to Noddy's surprise. Then he turned to Noddy.

"Get my bicycle off the back. I'll ride it, and you can stand behind me with the cat on your shoulder. Hurry now."

"Can't I—can't I say goodbye to my dear little car?" said Noddy, very sadly, lifting down the bicycle.

"No," said Big-Ears, sitting on the saddle, and handing the cat to Noddy. "Now—come along."

And away they rode on the bicycle, Big-Ears in front and Noddy behind him with the big cat purring on his shoulder. Poor Noddy! He had never felt so sad in his life. His dear little car! It didn't belong to him any more. It belonged to the wizard.

8. EVERYTHING'S RIGHT AGAIN!

THEY hadn't gone very far down the road when Big-Ears stopped. "Cheer up, little Noddy," he said. "*I* know some magic too, though I don't use it much nowadays. Hold the cat firmly. Now watch!" He drew a circle in the dust at his feet and stepped into it. He began singing some strange words—and then, to Noddy's enormous surprise, he began to hoot like a car! "Parp-parp-parp! Parp-parp! PARP! PARP-PARP!"

And almost at once there came an answering call. "PARP! PARP-PARP!"

"That—that sounds like *my* car!" said Noddy, his face shining with delight. "Oh, listen—I can hear it rattling down the hill—and there it is coming round the corner. But the wizard's in it, Big-Ears, the wizard's in it! *Now* what shall we do?"

EVERYTHING'S RIGHT AGAIN!

"Nothing," said Big-Ears. "The car knows what to do. There—what did I tell you?"

The little car stopped so very suddenly that it almost stood on its two front wheels—and whooosh! The wizard shot out into the road! He rolled over and over and over, talking at the top of his voice all the time.

The car drove quickly over to Noddy. Big-Ears got in with his cat, and Noddy threw the bicycle on to the back of the car. Then he jumped into the driver's seat and drove away at top speed. Big-Ears called out to the astonished Wily Wizard who was still sitting down in the road.

YOU'RE A GOOD FRIEND NODDY!

"I paid you sixpence for the cat, so we don't owe you anything. Did you think I'd be silly enough to let you have the car? Go back and make a spell to grow yourself a few brains, Wily!"

"Oh, Big-Ears, Big-Ears, I've got my little car back, after all!" said Noddy, too delighted for words. "I love my car just as much as you love your cat."

"And yet you gave it up so that I might have my dear old Whiskers back again," said Big-Ears, cuddling his cat. "If we weren't going at sixty miles an hour, Noddy, I'd hug you like a bear. You're the best friend I've ever had!"

"Oh, *Big-Ears!* You do say nice things," said Noddy, nodding his head joyfully. "Everything's right again, isn't it?"

EVERYTHING'S RIGHT AGAIN!

"Not quite," said Big-Ears. "I'm going to buy Tessie a new dress to make up for being cross with her—and I'm going to buy the Bumpy-Dog a big bone to make up for whacking him with my stick. And I'm going to give *another* party, but this time it will be for my very best friend, and I'll ask everyone."

"A party for *me?*" said Noddy. "Oh, Big-Ears, I was so sad, I thought everything was spoilt, but

it isn't. It's lovely to have friends when things go wrong, isn't it, Big-Ears? And I've got lots of friends so I'm very, very lucky!" And Noddy sang a joyful little song all the way home. Big-Ears joined in, and so did the cat. Even the little car said "Parp-parp" at the right moment.

"Oh, I'm very lucky,
 Because, you see,

YOU'RE A GOOD FRIEND NODDY!

So many people are friends with me!
And when I'm in trouble
And feeling sad,
There's always SOMEONE to make me glad.
'Parp-parp!' says my car
In its friendly way,
'Good morning!' says Big-Ears. 'It's such a nice day!'
'Meow!' says the cat,
And purrs on my knee,
And Tessie Bear's always as sweet as can be!
Miss Fluffy Cat smiles,
And the Tubby Bears too,
And Bumpy-Dog's loving the whole day through.
Oh, I'm VERY lucky,
Because, you see,
So many people are friends with me!"

We can't *help* being friends with you, Noddy. You're such a nice little fellow!

THE NODDY LIBRARY

1. NODDY GOES TO TOYLAND
2. HURRAH FOR LITTLE NODDY
3. NODDY AND HIS CAR
4. HERE COMES NODDY AGAIN!
5. WELL DONE NODDY!
6. NODDY GOES TO SCHOOL
7. NODDY AT THE SEASIDE
8. NODDY GETS INTO TROUBLE
9. NODDY AND THE MAGIC RUBBER
10. YOU FUNNY LITTLE NODDY
11. NODDY MEETS FATHER CHRISTMAS
12. NODDY AND TESSIE BEAR
13. BE BRAVE LITTLE NODDY!
14. NODDY AND THE BUMPY-DOG
15. DO LOOK OUT NODDY!
16. YOU'RE A GOOD FRIEND NODDY!
17. NODDY HAS AN ADVENTURE
18. NODDY GOES TO SEA
19. NODDY AND THE BUNKEY
20. CHEER UP LITTLE NODDY!
21. NODDY GOES TO THE FAIR
22. MR PLOD AND LITTLE NODDY
23. NODDY AND THE TOOTLES
24. NODDY AND THE AEROPLANE